DIRTY LITTLE SECRETS

Life, Love, Adoption & Addiction

Elle Soto

Copyright © 2021 Elle Soto

All rights reserved

The characters and events portrayed in this book are fictitious. Any similarity to real persons, living or dead, is coincidental and not intended by the author.

No part of this book may be reproduced, or stored in a retrieval system, or transmitted in any form or by any means, electronic, mechanical, photocopying, recording, or otherwise, without express written permission of the publisher.

ISBN: 9798731618182

Cover design by: Art Painter
Library of Congress Control Number: 2018675309
Printed in the United States of America

For Brian and Melita, naturally.

**Dirty Little Secrets:
Life, Love, Adoption, and Addiction**

*You live you learn,
You love you learn,
You cry you learn,
You lose you learn,
You bleed you learn,
You scream you learn.*

*– Alanis Morrisette, "You Learn"
Jagged Little Pill*

INTRODUCTION

"Dirty Little Secrets: Life, Love, Adoption and Addiction" is a collection of genuine short stories beggining in Elle's early childhood in Canada throughout her years into adulthood in Texas. Her adoption and addiction issues are addressed throughout this journey as she discusses each one of life's lessons. From growing up with a badass sister, to the grief she experiences after losing the love of her life and then her sister, as well as her addiction to prescription pain pills. And finally, her recovery.

CHAPTER EIGHTEEN	48
CHAPTER NINETEEN	51
CHAPTER TWENTY	54
CHAPTER TWENTY-ONE	56
CHAPTER TWENTY-TWO	58
CHAPTER TWENTY-THREE	60
CHAPTER TWENTY-FOUR	62
CHAPTER TWENTY-FIVE	66
CHAPTER TWENTY-SIX	70
CHAPTER TWENTY-SEVEN	74
CHAPTER TWENTY-EIGHT	77
CHAPTER THIRTY	79
CHAPTER TWENTY-NINE	81
CHAPTER THIRTY-ONE	84
CHAPTER THIRTY-TWO	87
Acknowledgement	91
About The Author	93

CONTENTS

Title Page	1
Copyright	2
Dedication	3
Introduction	7
CHAPTER ONE	9
CHAPTER TWO	11
CHAPTER THREE	14
CHAPTER FOUR	16
CHAPTER FIVE	19
CHAPTER SIX	21
CHAPTER SEVEN	24
CHAPTER EIGHT	26
CHAPTER NINE	28
CHAPTER TEN	30
CHAPTER ELEVEN	32
CHAPTER TWELVE	34
CHAPTER THIRTEEN	37
CHAPTER FOURTEEN	40
CHAPTER FIFTEEN	42
CHAPTER SIXTEEN	44
CHAPTER SEVENTEEN	46

CHAPTER ONE

I'll keep you my dirty little secret (Dirty little secret) Don't tell anyone, or you'll be just another regret (Just another regret, hope that you can keep it) My dirty little secret

– The All-American Rejects, "Dirty Little Secret"

<u>Dirty Little Secret</u>
<u>2004</u>
<u>Toronto</u>

I was fortunate enough to know my birth mother, Patricia, for 6 years before she succumbed to pancreatic cancer. I was only able to spend a very brief amount of time with her during a visit in 1999 since I was living in Texas, but I had grown to love her all the same. Although I am grateful for the 6 years that I did have, I was sad that I wouldn't have a chance for us to grow closer. It's really weird to see your mother for the first time at 29. I realize that the environment has a lot to do with how a child turns out, but there is something to be said about genetics as well. For example, people said we walked the same way. We both loved gardening, the same type of music, a little wine now and then. I don't know; it's just surreal seeing people you resemble for the first time in your life at 29. As warm and genuine as she was, there were still situations that really hit home for me just how much I was never really intended to exist, like her funeral.

I flew to Toronto for her funeral simply because I wanted to show respect for the woman that gave me life as well as be there for my father who was understandably devastated after 35 years of marriage. At my dad's house that evening, I called my Aunt Sharon, my mother's sister, to let her know I was there and would be attending the funeral the next day. Her reaction was bizarre, and the conversation went something like this:

"Hi Aunt Sharon, it's Lynda. I'm here for the funeral tomorrow."
"You're HERE?!"
"Well, yeah, of course."
"I guess it's too late now."
"Um. Come again?" I replied in confusion.
"Never mind. Nothing we can do about it now."
"Is there a problem?" I asked.
"So. How's John? Is he drinking?" she replied ignoring my question.

This was news to me because I had never known my dad to be much of a drinker, maybe the occasional beer. Still, I thought to myself that if he was going to drink, well gosh, now would probably be the perfect occasion. I decided to end this conversation, "Okay then, see you tomorrow, I guess."

Apparently, there was a majority of Patricia's family and friends who still didn't know about me. In my defense, it's not like I was planning on announcing my existence to the entire church, but as I sat next to my dad in the first pew at the service with about 200 eyes plastered on me, I felt as though I was wearing a sign around my neck that read, "Baby Girl Jones," I knew I was a dirty little secret when I was born. I just didn't realize that 34 years later, I still was.

CHAPTER TWO

I live my life like there's no tomorrow
And all I've got, I had to steal
'Least I don't need to beg or borrow

– Van Halen, "Running with the Devil"

<u>Lifesavers</u>
<u>1976</u>
<u>Peterborough, Ontario</u>

Melita, my soon-to-be sister, was having a visit with us before the adoption, basically to make sure we all liked each other. She had stayed for dinner and it was getting dark, so we were taking her back to her foster home. Before us, Melita was living with another family in Toronto. They had planned on adopting her, but it turns out she was pretty high maintenance, and they ultimately decided that it just wasn't a good fit for either party. Although a necessary step when adopting older children, think about how that makes the kid feel? Nah. No thank you, we'll pass on you. You're just not worth the trouble. I mean, fuck you know? My mom once told me that the mother of this family Melita was with had a nervous breakdown because of her. Add that to the mix, too. This family, we'll call them *The Smiths*, just didn't understand her.

They already had eight-year-old twin boys, and the boys were not excited about Melita's arrival. Apparently, there was a lot of animosity between the twins and Melita. I'll be honest; Melita had said they were a couple of little assholes. But what kid that's been kicked around from home to home before their tenth birthday wouldn't be a little troubled? It actually would have been a lot scarier if she wasn't affected by all that had happened to her so far. They had chosen her as a daughter and stuck her in a frilly pink room with a closet full of dresses. No. Uh-uh. She wasn't having any of that. She had spent most of her life so far in an orphanage on a farm in Newfoundland. Her best friend was her pet pig, and so she was not really the frilly pink type, but more of a tomboy.

Since she was stuck in a pink bedroom and also had the two little assholes conspiring against her, she ran away. A lot! So, I guess between the running away, fighting with the twins, and just a host of other shenanigans, it wasn't working out. Oh, and the nervous breakdown Mrs. Smith had was blamed on nine-year-old Melita, as well.

So as Melita, my dad, and myself are standing under the dim light on the Smith's front porch just having rang the doorbell and returning Melita home for the night; something falls out of my sister's coat sleeve onto the ground. What is that? I'm squinting when my dad quickly picks it up. Oh! Lifesavers, a brand new roll of Lifesavers just like the one Dad keeps on his dresser. '*Huh, what a coincidence.*' I'm thinking innocently. My dad picked up the Lifesavers roll quickly and then whispered to Melita, "We'll talk about this later." I'm standing there a bit confused due to my six-year-old brain thinking, '*What's there to talk about? You both like Lifesavers?*'
We had a couple of visits before officially adopting Melita. I was counting down the days until her arrival. I had always wanted a sister and if the twins didn't want her obviously, I sure did!

"Melita, come sit on my lap." my dad said one day soon after she arrived. She did, and then he began speaking to her, "You know, Melita, this is your home now. Everything we have is now also yours. There's no need to take or steal anything from here because you are welcome to it all." He repeated himself, emphasizing each word so she would get it, "This Is Now Your Home."

My dad seemed like a much kinder man when we were in Canada for some reason. I really had to give him props for speaking this way to her about it because it worked. She never, not once, ran away from home or stole again after joining our family. She, finally, truly had found a home.

CHAPTER THREE

Take this pink ribbon off my eyes
I'm exposed and it's no big surprise
Don't you think I know exactly where I stand?
The world is forcing me to hold your hand

– No Doubt, "Just a Girl"

<u>Even a Badass Needs Love</u>
<u>1977</u>
<u>Peterborough, Ontario</u>

A few months after my parents adopted my sister, Melita, she became really sad one night. This is one of my earliest memories with her. We shared a room, and I could hear her crying in her bed, so I got up, walked to my parent's bedroom, and said, "Mom. Mama. Mama, Melita's crying," and stumbled back to bed. My mom walked into our room, got my sister up, and they went to the living room. I was six years old when my parents adopted Melita who was already 10, and we were her third home. Can you imagine? I mean, the insecurity a child must feel not expecting their home to last? All a kid has to himself is usually his/her room, and she had no sense of belonging anywhere. I was already awake (my mom claimed I never slept as a child because I was worried I'd miss out on something, and that's still kind of true) and could hear soft murmuring coming from the living room, so I got up again and tiptoed down the hall to quietly peek in on them.

My mother sat in a chair gently rocking my 10-year-old sister like a baby, whereas the tears continued silently down her cheeks. Mom hummed a familiar lullaby as she rocked this big kid like a baby. She looked so large on my mom's lap, all arms and legs. We didn't have to ask her what was wrong. I mean, what in her head at this time could have been right? I knew we would be her last home, but I don't think she realized that for quite some time. Probably once we made it to Texas, she figured we were stuck with her, and by God, she was right.

CHAPTER FOUR

Round and round
With love we'll find a way just give it time
Round and round
What comes around goes around

– Ratt, "Round and Round"

<u>Merry-Go-Round</u>
<u>1977</u>
<u>Winnipeg, Manitoba</u>

My Nana, my dad's mother, was Ukrainian and one of the sweetest women I have ever known. She was short, a bit heavyset, and had a strong Ukrainian accent, and she was a Jehovah's Witness, so no television or presents. Once, we bought her a television, so we could watch it when we visited. We were sitting in the living room, watching some show but the reception wasn't great, so she looks up for a minute and says, "The trash is blurry." God love her. She had one of those really cool old three-story homes and rented out the rooms on the second and third floors to tenants, so I always had to sleep in a cot in the corner of the kitchen when we visited. I only understood every other word she said to me because it was mostly Ukrainian, which of course, I am not fluent in. I know she was constantly pushing food in front of me, so most of the time I would just look at her and say, "No, no really, it's okay Nana. I'm not hungry but thank you!" And she would only pick up on the "thank you" so we ate a lot during our visits.

On one such visit in 1977, we were preparing to fly home to Toronto later in the day. Melita and I had our squeaky clean "travel" clothes on and were instructed to stay clean before it was time to leave. "No problem. We can do that," we said as we walked down the street to the muddy park. Melita always had a way of never being "it" during our childhood games. I was always doing the chasing in tag or the finding in hide-n-seek. This meant, of course, that I was the one pushing her on the merry-go-round. I pushed her faster and faster as I ran and pushed as hard as I could. Then suddenly, I was down.

I must admit that I am extremely accident-prone. Anytime there's an opportunity for a clumsy fall, why, I'm your girl. As I lay there in the muddy water, it occurred to me that I was about to get in some kind of big trouble. Fortunately for me, Melita wasn't willing for us to go down quite so fast. She explained her plan to get us out of this since we still had a good 4 or 5 hours before we had to leave. Amazingly, we actually got away with it this time.

We approached Nana's house from the backyard sneaking in the back door to the basement which of course had laundry facilities. Ancient facilities, but we made it work. Nana had one of those old washers from the 1930s complete with a wringer. Of course, there was no dryer since she always hung her laundry on the line to dry. She also had trunks of vintage clothing and hats from the 30s and 40s, and it wasn't unusual for us to play dress-up with her old wardrobe. Step one was to get out of my muddy clothes and wash them. Step two was to play dress-up while said clothes are laundering. The only problem was how to dry my clothes. We couldn't put them on the line because it would be too obvious, so we hung them on the metal fence that was around the side of the house. Although this was a risky move, those clothes had to dry! Melita and I kept playing in the backyard in order to keep an eye on my clothing when my mother walked into the backyard, and unintentionally gave me my very first stress headache.

"Sid! Sid! Come see how cute the girls look! Let's take pictures!" *'Um... huh. Here goes nothing,'* I thought with crossed fingers. We ended up getting lucky and neither my mom nor my dad noticed my freshly laundered travel outfit hanging on the fence behind them as we posed for the picture after picture. I still have these pictures and laugh every time I spot my jeans hanging on the fence in the background.

CHAPTER FIVE

Oh Canada, glorious and free
We stand on guard; we stand on guard for thee
Oh Canada, we stand on guard for thee

– Oh Canada, Canadian National Anthem

<u>Canadian Coins & Candy</u>
<u>January 1978</u>
<u>Toronto, Ontario</u>

Our parents had announced that we would be moving to "The States," specifically Texas. Since I was seven and in Canada, I pictured rodeos and cacti, so I thought, *'Sure, great. Let's move to Texas.'* I was always up for an adventure and you know what they say about Canada—it's sort of like a really nice loft apartment that overlooks an awesome party down below. Melita and I had piggy banks and had decided to blow all our Canadian coins before moving to the States. Because, you know, it didn't occur to us that we could convert it to American currency. Besides, we thought obviously, they probably barter or something for everything since it's entirely desert in Texas. We really believed this.
We lived in Toronto at the time in a modest brick three-bedroom home and walked to school which was located directly behind our house, so at 7 and 11 years old, we were perfectly capable of walking to school alone. But. But, we were instructed by our parents to never, ever cross the busy intersection without one of them. So, of course, there was a shop located directly across the busy intersection from our school. We had this Canadian

money just burning a hole in our pocket and were leaving Canada soon, FOREVER! We really had no other choice but to cross the busy intersection to spend our hard-earned treasure, on candy, of course. In fact, this was quickly becoming a daily habit for us.

One day, my sister and I walked across the busy intersection with our hoard of candy, back toward school when we looked up and ran smack dab into my mother. She was onto us and the jig was up. Busted. Her eyes grew huge with anger, and then she wanted to know where we got the money for the candy. "Oh that," Melita said casually, "We're spending all of our Canadian money before we move," as if her explanation suddenly brought everything to light. I then contributed, "Yeah, on *candy*" to really drive the point home. My mom took a deep breath, took our candy, and instructed us to go back to school, and said that "we would discuss this when your father gets home." Well shit, Mom. That kind of changes things, I remember thinking.

As Melita and I walked back to school, somber and candyless, we came up with what I thought was a brilliant plan! If we're waiting for Dad to come home to give us a beating, why, let's not go home. Perfect! No matter that it was January in Ontario. So, after school that day, my sister and I just walked the neighborhood streets. Great plan! At one point when it started to get dark, we actually spotted our mother out walking the same streets looking for us and crying, and shamefully we hid from her behind a large snowdrift. I still feel bad about this. Two hours later, it was getting very dark, and we were tired and hungry, so we decided to go home and take our beatings.

CHAPTER SIX

*Since I was born they couldn't hold me down
Another misfit kid, another burned out town
I never played by the rules, I never really cared
My nasty reputation takes me everywhere*

– Skid Row, "Youth Gone Wild"

<u>Italian Girls</u>
<u>1979</u>
<u>Duncanville, Texas</u>

My sister, the aforementioned badass, was always getting into fights with the Italian girls in the neighborhood. I think it was merely a coincidence they were Italian, but they were the "tough girls" in our neighborhood, along with Melita, of course. And I'm not talking about arguing or simple name-calling. I'm talking about good old knockdown, fistfight, brawls. Melita was 13 or 14 at that time and would pummel any chick that had a crush on whoever she was into at the moment. I never really understood this concept, but she was fervent about it. I'd ask Melita, "How does beating up other girls make the boy like you?" She'd reply, "That's just how it is, Lynda. Don't worry about it." I wasn't worried, I just didn't understand the dynamics of such a situation.

Often, during the school day, some strange kid I'd never met before would run up to me and exclaim, "Hey, your sister's fighting Antoinette today at 3:30 at the park!" Oh, yeah? Sounds about right to me. They would run up to me and announce it like it's the next best Monster Truck Rally in history, "Sunday! Sunday! Sunday Only! At Meadowglen Drive Only! Smoke inside! Punch a baby! Smoke inside! Watch two teenage girls beat the crap out of each other! Sunday! Sunday! Sunday!" I'm not exaggerating when I tell you that at about 3:15 if you looked outside, you could see groups of kids, of all various ages, heading toward the park just down the street chanting, "Fight, fight, fight!" I'd go out and join the group, walking closely behind Melita who was leading the blood-thirsty mob. Once the mob and the two young ladies in question made it to the park, they'd begin circling each other like angry prey. The crowd would choose which side they were on backing up whomever they were routing for. Melita's side was always larger because she always won. Both girls always had rings on all their fingers so that their punches would inflict as much damage as possible. How ladylike and lovely! Melita always took the first punch. This was her strategy because she believed being on the offensive gave her the upper hand. She wasn't wrong.

There was this one fight that actually got a bit out of hand. The girl she was supposed to fight, Angela, didn't show up for the fight at the park (a wise move on her part), but we all knew where she lived, so the blood-thirsty mob followed Melita to Angela's house just a bit further down the street. This crazy group of kids starts up with the chanting again, "Fight, fight, fight!" So, Angela strolls out onto her front yard, on her own property, and as Melita's usual fashion, my sister immediately throws the first punch, and this poor girl is down; Melita was pummeling her. Suddenly, Angela's front door busts wide open and her Mom runs over to the two girls and throws my sister off of her daughter. Dude, a parent was there! Nobody counted on that so the mob split up drastically and quickly as everyone ran home so they wouldn't get in trouble, including Melita and myself.

I guess about 30 minutes later, there's a loud cop knock on my door. You know the one, you can always tell when it's the police. I say to Melita, "Go to your room, I'll cover for you!" Right? I'm nine years old so I'm thinking I got this. I open the door to a cop, the Mother, and most of the blood-thirsty mob on my front lawn,

"Hello, officer. How can I help you?"

"Can you please get your sister for me?"

"Oh officer, no can do. She's not here, of course."

Immediately after that, my sister appears at the door, figuring she might as well face the music I guess, making me look like the liar that I was. Nice. Our mother also arrived home from work at about this time. Both mothers and the extremely patient policeman agreed that we all just needed to leave each other alone, and Mom tried to explain to the cop that I was only trying to protect my sister, but I still felt like a total dumbass.

CHAPTER SEVEN

Beauty's where you find it,
Not just where you bump and grind it.
– Madonna, "Vogue"

<u>French Whore</u>
<u>1980</u>
<u>Duncanville, Texas</u>

I think most of us agree, labeling people is wrong, but in the 1980s, there wasn't a whole lot of talk about that yet, so labeled I was. One spring day in 1980, I stared in the mirror and thought, "Wow, I look really different with make-up on. Older, too." and my hair had two French braids running through it. I thought I was looking pretty hot! My neighbor and a dear friend to this day, Pam, is four years older than me and said I had a good face for make-up, whatever that meant. She had spent a good couple of hours working on my hair and applying layer after layer of make-up, and I felt like her masterpiece! Well, rock on. I had a ton of cosmetics on my face as I walked home in a dainty fashion, exhibiting my newfound beauty.
I opened the front door, pranced inside, and sat down beside my mother crossing my legs like a lady on the sofa, batting my mascaraed eyelashes at her. Mom was reading her tabloid newspaper and didn't even raise her eyes from whatever she was reading when she said to me, "You look like a French whore," totally deflating my prissy mood. Thank you, Mother! I immediately walked to the bathroom to scrub all the layers of makeup off my face, but I did keep my hair in the French braids for a couple of

days. Dang it.

A few years later, my mom and I are waiting in the car to pick up Melita from school. We spot her walking down the sidewalk talking to her friends as she makes her way to our car at Trinity High School. My mom and I are just watching and waiting for her when Mom said to me, "Well Lynda, you got the brains and she got the beauty." Is that supposed to be a compliment because all I could focus on was that Melita was the pretty one? I mean, what was I? Chopped liver? So, for a while, I thought I was ugly, and Melita felt stupid. Neither was true of course, but what parents say really resonates with their kids. Labeling is a pet peeve of mine now. If we're going to argue or debate, no name-calling; let's fight fair or not at all.

CHAPTER EIGHT

It's beginning to look a lot like Christmas
Toys in every store
It's the prettiest sight to see
Is the holly that will be on your own front door

– Dean Martin, "It's Beginning to Look Like Christmas"

<u>Christmas Eve</u>
<u>December 24, 1981</u>
<u>Duncanville, Texas</u>

It was getting dark, so I was running home from my neighbor's house on Christmas Eve. Melita was still there visiting with her best friend, Pam. I entered the front door of the modest home where we resided with my mother anticipating the warm sounds and smells of Christmas.

But as I walked through the dark house, it looked as if nobody was home. When I made my way to the dining room, I noticed my mom. She was on the floor with an empty bottle in her hand. Actually, it was an empty bottle of peach schnapps. Ew, yuck. I stopped suddenly when I saw her there, sprawled out on the dining room floor. "Are you sick, Mom?" I asked rather worriedly. I think she was trying to reply, but I couldn't understand a word she was saying on account of her obvious inebriation. She managed to get out some gargles and moans as she literally crawled on her hands and knees through the dining room, the kitchen, down the hall, and into her bedroom where she slammed the door behind her using her foot. Merry Christmas.

I was 11 years old at that time, so for me Christmas was pretty much the most important day of the year, and I was upset. I also astutely recognized that something was just not right with my mom, and that thought kicked around in my brain as well. I ran back over to the neighbor's house, tears streaming down my face, to fetch Melita. She'll know what to do surely, I thought. I pulled Melita aside and began explaining to my sister that something was seriously up with Mom. Melita had been through much worse and so this to her was just not a big deal.

"She'll be fine in the morning, Lynda. Jeez." Melita told me, trying to help me stop crying.

"But it's Christmas," I replied to her in earnest desperation.

"Well. Just suck it up, Lynda."

We spent the night that Christmas Eve at the neighbor's house. I remember drifting off to sleep, hoping and praying things would go back to normal by the morning like some Christmas miracle. I ran home in the morning and burst open the front door. Nothing. No stocking, no presents, no mother.

CHAPTER NINE

If you don't know what it's like, you don't have a clue
If you did, you'd find yourselves doing the same thing too
Breaking the law
Breaking the law

– Judas Priest, "Breaking the Law"

<u>Get Out of Jail Free Card</u>
<u>1983</u>
<u>Dallas, Texas</u>

"You better pull over, Mom." I pleaded. My mother had brought me with her to eat dinner, and apparently drink, at her friend's restaurant that had just opened in Dallas. I remember how amazing the homemade Mexican food tasted and that they were super generous with the tequila which explained why we were being pulled over by not one, but two, Dallas police cars.

As my mother drove us home through Dallas, I suddenly realized that she was lit. Great! I'm 13 and we're going to die tonight, I thought to myself because my mom is seriously impaired. I was observing how she couldn't even keep the car in one lane when I saw the blue lights and heard the siren. Shit. This was happening. It was a female officer who approached our car to speak to my mom. She aimed her flashlight in the car and then on me when she stopped and said that phrase to my mother that nobody wants to hear, "Ma'am, please step out of the car."

I'm not exactly sure what was said as I watched them speaking in the rearview mirror. All I kept thinking was that my dad was going to completely lose his shit if my mom gets arrested, and I'm with her. And I actually couldn't blame him this time. I kept watching and at one point actually saw my mother get on her knees and put up her right hand up in the air as if she was making a vow to the nice lady cop that she was NOT, as God as her witness, drunk. Ughhhhhh. Unfortunately, her words contradicted her behavior. I could see the officer losing her patience, but they continued talking.

The officer then walked to her car and spoke to someone on her radio for a good five minutes. When she returned to my mom, they exchanged a few more words; then, each of them returned to their respective vehicles. Um. What the? Oh. My. God. How did she get out of this? I can't say with absolute certainty who the officer spoke to, but Mom was dating the Chief of Police for the city she lived in at the time. I'm just saying.

Mom opened the car door and sat down in the driver's seat. I looked at her waiting for her to say something. All she said as she started the car was that the officer was right about one thing. No matter what, having me with her while she drinks is never, ever okay. As my mom drove and spoke, she actually seemed to sober up.

CHAPTER TEN

Why, oh why, must it be this way?
Before you can read me
You gotta learn how to see me, I said

– En Vogue, "Free Your Mind"

Karma's a Bitch
1983
Euless, Texas

My father was a tight-fisted control freak with a short fuse. My sister, for whatever reason, had some sort of self-destructive streak and never missed an opportunity to push this man's buttons. She had a real gift for lighting his short fuse and sending him into a blinding, hot rage. I am in no way suggesting physical abuse is ever deserved, I'm just saying Melita was a smart girl and knew just what to say, or not to say, to set him off and she did so quite deliberately.

One evening, Dad came home from work in one of his famous moods. Melita was standing next to the dining room table folding laundry, and I was sitting on the living room floor practicing my clarinet so my sheet music was spread all over the floor. My dad stood over me and started yelling about the mess. He was getting louder and closer to me so I put my hands up to him in a defensive mode. Well, for some reason, this struck my sister as hilarious, and so she started to laugh. While cracking up, a corner of the towel she was folding barely touched the ground. Uh-oh! Hold on

tight now. My dad's eyes suddenly glowed red and steam started coming out of his ears as he turned his attention to Melita.
"You did that on purpose! Get that towel off the floor," he bellowed at her.

What Melita did next still shocks and amazes me. To this day, she was and always will remain, the biggest badass I've ever known. She later told me it just happened and she was powerless to stop it.

She popped Dad with the towel she was folding. Oh fuck! In an instant, he was chasing her around the table, round and round, back and forth, until he literally climbed over the table to get to her. And when he got to her, he wrapped his hands around her neck and began to choke her. I became so frightened, I screamed as loudly as I could, "Dad, Stop," and he did. My sister seized the opportunity to flee and ran to the front door opening and exiting as quickly as possible. But Dad was fast and angry and managed to actually kick her in the ass as she ran out the door and into the night.

The next day while sitting on the couch, I glanced over at my dad. He was sitting in his chair with his legs crossed reading the newspaper. I couldn't help but notice his big toe and grinned. The entire toe was black, swollen, and had to be broken. I thought to myself, "Good. Karma's a bitch."

CHAPTER ELEVEN

It all keeps adding up
I think I'm cracking up
Am I just paranoid,
Or am I just stoned?

– Green Day, "Basket Case"

<u>Flipping Out</u>
<u>1984</u>
<u>Euless, Texas</u>

Between 1982 and 1986, Melita and I lived in a tiny apartment with my dad, a dog, and a cat. There was a large empty field outside our front door so this is where we took our dog, Lady, to do her business. The first 30 feet or so was always kept neatly mowed by property management, but the further out you went the higher and crazier the grass and weeds became. Lady, who was really old, would pop a squat as close to our front door as possible. Probably in an effort to avoid paying a pet deposit, my dad would go outside and "flip" the shit to the outer field with the tall grass. He'd walk from turd pile to turd pile with the scooper from the litter box and flip the shit. What can I say? The man had a system.

One evening, my sister and I sat on the patio talking and catching up on our day when my dad came strolling by litter box scooper in hand. As per his usual routine, my dad begins flipping dog poop into the meadow. Melita and I are suddenly struck by this ridiculous-looking act and realize, well, it's funny. We're giggling to ourselves when suddenly Melita exclaims loudly, "Who IS that strange man flipping shit?" Oh, come on, Melita, he's going to kill you for that, I'm thinking as I immediately begin scrambling for the door before he can turn around and see us.

Dad suddenly stops his shit-flipping duties, stands up, and slowly turns around to look at us. I start having a panic attack, but much to my surprise, he begins to laugh. Wait, what now? Yes, I look at him, and by some miracle, he was actually laughing. I guess it just goes to show you that even an asshole can have a good day, a lesson learned that has always served me well.

CHAPTER TWELVE

*You can choose from phantom fears
And kindness that can kill
I will choose the path that's clear
I will choose free will.*

– Rush, "Free Will"

<u>The Power Struggle</u>
<u>1985</u>
<u>Euless, Texas</u>

I may have mentioned, by this point, that my dad was a major control freak. This was his biggest fault, hands down because it seemed all his anger came from this one festering issue buried deep within him like he unintentionally carried it around with him. All I knew is on this day, however, is that he was royally pissed. A real "my way or the highway" kind of dude. "No" was his favorite word so there was no point in asking for anything. You get the picture. At least he was predictable.

One evening as Dad arrived home from work, he walked into the apartment just as Melita was hanging up the phone. Since she was grounded from the phone, she tried to explain to Dad that she had merely answered the phone and it was for me so she was just hanging up as he entered through the door. That is the only reason she was on the phone. As usual, the situation escalated quickly. Suddenly my Dad's screaming at Melita, "Well, you answered the phone on purpose didn't you?" Melita sighed and said blankly,

"Okay, yeah, sure." Her sarcasm did not go unnoticed. He took off his belt and instructed her to stick out her hand, palms up, just like we used to do for the nuns in Catholic school. So Melita stuck out her hand.

He asked her much more slowly this time,
"Did you. Do that. On purpose?"
"Yes. Yes, I did."
"*Thwack!*" the belt whipped across her palm.

This went on for 30 more thwacks. I know because I sat there in the hall listening and counting each blow from the belt. I wanted to burst into the room and tell her to just say, "NO!" already, but I knew that would only make it worse for one or both of us. So, I sat silently outside the door, willing her to stop. And finally, after 31 thwacks she submitted and whimpered, "No."

It was during one of these super fucked up moments when I would wonder why, on God's green Earth, did he ever sign up to be a parent? I mean, it was a very deliberate and somewhat expensive act for my parents to acquire a baby through adoption. And, he clearly found no joy in parenting. I would later discover my mom had baby fever and that he thought it would "help things" if he got her one. The new wife thought I needed to know this for some reason as if being adopted at all doesn't at some basic level generate feelings of abandonment. But I am grateful for it. I exist today thanks to adoption. I also have the invoice Dad's attorney sent him to process the adoption. It had cost him about $243 to push me through the adoption process in a court system, in Canada in 1970. This invoice is stapled to my adoption papers as if it's some sort of warranty on his purchase of one daughter. It actually does make me feel like I was purchased, a little anyway, which isn't the best feeling in the world.

My adoptive parents, Sid and Mary, were married at the City Hall in Paris, France. My dad was in the American Air Force, even though he was Canadian at the time. He did this in case he should ever decide to move to the States, which he did. He met my mom in Germany while she was nannying her way out of poverty. I think from a very early start, my dad was taught that he was, for all intents and purposes, the shit. And he owned it. My nana would always say to me at dinner in a hushed tone, "Serve the men first."

"Okay, Nana, but isn't it customary to serve ladies first?" I would reply.

"What? No. Nooo. Men work hard all day, for us!"

I got what she was saying, but couldn't resist messing with her, just a little.

"I don't even know those guys, Nana? How could they be working hard for me?"

But, she would just start mumbling about how awful it was that I wasn't yet married at the ripe old age of 15, shaking her head in disappointment. My point is, Dad had a pretty inflated ego which was only perpetuated by his mother. And it enraged him when people didn't do exactly what he wanted, so Melita was always pissing him smooth off. Thirty-one blows by the belt; she was one badass bitch.

CHAPTER THIRTEEN

Higher than high, feelin' just right
Call it Heavy Metal
Desperation in a red line,
Call it Heavy Metal noise

– Sammy Hagar, "Heavy Metal"

<u>Heavy Metal</u>
<u>1986–1987</u>
<u>Texas</u>

I am incredibly happy that I was born in 1970 because it meant that I was in my teenage prime during the 1980s. The 80s truly had to be the best decade for a teenager. This was the decade of Arena Rock, and my friends and I embraced this head-banging scene with open arms. Simply put, good times. Good freaking times. There's just nothing like it today where you can't even go to the grocery store without wearing an annoying mask. This drastic change in my style and behavior was not at all too pleasing to my father, however. Previously, I had been a pretty good kid. But the lure of sex, drugs, and rock and roll was just too good for me to pass upon. One day, I started bleaching and perming my hair as blonde and large as I could possibly make it, my make-up became darker and heavier, and the clothing—so freaking cool we thought, even though we resembled ladies of the evening by this point. We didn't care because the sluttier looking you were, the cooler you were, so thigh-high boots and spandex were aplenty in the 1980s.

But the biggest draw for me and all these changes was the music, the Arena Rock Concerts. I saw all the good ones, many of them more than once: Van Halen, Ozzy Ozbourne, Motley Crue, Iron Maiden, KISS, etc. And you could smoke cigarettes inside rock concerts during this time, so there was a *lot* of pot being passed around everywhere, especially if you had floor tickets, which, of course, I usually did. What could be better for adolescent girls? My clarinet just couldn't compete.

During a KISS concert in probably 1986 sometime, at Tarrant County Convention Center in downtown Fort Worth, my friend Tricia and I were hanging our scantily clad, heavily made-up selves off the lower balcony as close to the stage as possible when Paul Stanley called us out, obviously noticing that we were looking to get noticed. You would have thought we had won the lottery at the reaction we received. It was just awesome. I mean, come on. Suddenly, the spotlight was on us, and an entire gaggle of head-banging teenage boys was encouraging us to jump onto the floor, "Come on ladies! We'll catch you, really!" Tricia and I looked at each other with a raised eyebrow but thought better of it at the last moment. We didn't really care about hurting ourselves, but we didn't want to miss the rest of the concert on the off chance security got to us, priorities being what they were back then. Besides, as previously mentioned, I'm not the most graceful person in the world.

During the 1980s, in Dallas, in the very unsafe hell-like heat of the summer, usually July, the local rock station, Q102, would hold an annual, day-long, outdoor heavy metal rock concerts, and they were each called, "The Q102 Texxas Jamm," held at the Cotton Bowl in south Dallas, the old Fair Park area. Nothing like 80,000 head-bangers drunk, on drugs, banging heads, in a heavily crowded, one hundred degree, all day long, heavy metal concert. Sure kids! Go ahead, have fun! I went every year. Sometimes with my sister, sometimes with Tricia, sometimes with a boyfriend, but my attendance was always mandatory as far as I was concerned. Man, sounds strange I know, but they were so fun.

One year, I went with Melita and Pam. Pam became a little overcome by the heat (and alcohol and drugs), and so we dropped her at the first aid tent before heading to the next show. I know, such good friends, but we were young and immature and most likely jacked up at the time. I can't even remember who was coming to the stage next, but I think it was The Scorpions, and somehow Melita and I had been pushed into the front of the crowd and honestly couldn't have gotten out of there if we tried, the crowd was so thick. About this time, whatever drugs I had just ingested began to take effect and I started "tripping" for lack of a better term. So, it's a hundred degrees or so, and I'm tripping, and Melita and I are trapped in this crowd. Since it was so hot, and again as previously mentioned—the sluttier the attire, the better; we both had shorts on and bikini tops. It was hot after all. Melita had a short sleeve blouse tied around her waist thankfully because suddenly some dude snatches the back of her bikini top, ripping it clean off of her! Melita had been holding me up due to my drug trip, so I suddenly fell to the ground, but when I sort of came to, all I could see was her womanhood bouncing around, and then she was socking that guy square in the face, but he somehow got away into the thick crowd with her bikini top. Luckily, she still had the shirt around her waist to wear. See? Just plain FUN.

CHAPTER FOURTEEN

Mental wounds not healing
Who and what's to blame
I'm going off the rails on a crazy train

– Ozzy Ozbourne, "Crazy Train"

<u>The Will</u>
<u>1986</u>
<u>Fort Worth, Texas</u>

One day, when I was 16 years old and six months pregnant, my dad called me and asked me to meet him for dinner with him and his lovely new wife. I can understand why that might seem like a perfectly normal request for most people. But this was largely out of character for Dad, especially because it was at a restaurant. I'm not quite sure how to begin to express exactly how cheap he was; there may be no words. For example, this man would walk around with a bag of apples when we went to the mall (Malls were big in the 1980s. This is where teens socialized before all the social media). So rather than being conned by the restaurants in the food court into buying, you know, *food*, we would walk around with our bag of apples like some apple-picking weirdos. I honestly usually preferred to just stay home.

As I was saying, I was 16. He had also invited my sister to dinner; she was 20 at the time. We were both a bit confused, but intrigued, by his invitation. Melita and I were not making excellent life choices at this point is one way to put it. I was 16 and pregnant long before MTV made it popular, and Melita was living with and supporting some cowboy 10 years her senior. Still, as I drove to the restaurant that night, I thought, "Well, maybe this is a good thing?"

It was not a good thing. I soon discovered this as Melita and I sat across the table from my dad and the new wife. My dad began talking, "Girls. The reason I've brought you here tonight is to let you both know you are officially out of the will." (Gee, I wonder who is in the will, I thought as I cut my eyes at the new wife). Wow. Thanks SO much for dinner. He actually took us out to dinner to make sure we understood the full ramifications of our actions. He went on to explain how disappointed he was in us, and until we made changes (dump the losers), he would continue to be disappointed and we would remain out of his will.

This whole "will" concept was mostly just confusing to me for the following reasons:

1. Will? What will? I've NEVER even heard about said will until today.
2. If there had been a will, we would never have expected to be in it.
3. I'm sure if there had been a way to get all Dad's cash and bury it with him, that would have been in the will.

But 12 years later, he kept his promise. When Dad passed from colon cancer in April 1998, he left everything to the new wife; I'll always refer to her this way. She promptly sold their house and moved herself and all his money to Arkansas to go live with her family. He had left strict instructions that there should be no funeral or memorial of any kind because he claimed it was just a waste of money. I was 28 when he died and planted an azalea bush in my front yard as my own personal memorial to him. This was my first experience with a loss of life, and I struggled with it, but unfortunately, it was just the first of many to come.

CHAPTER FIFTEEN

She got legs, she knows how to use them
She never begs, she knows how to choose them

– ZZ Top, "Legs"

<u>High Heels</u>
<u>1987</u>
<u>Euless, Texas</u>

The thing about high heels is that during a spousal argument, they can be used as a weapon as my mother demonstrated one day while working at the family business. My parents had divorced in 1978 but continued to work together since they both had a lot of money invested in the family business which, at the time, was a car rental franchise. My dad paid my sister and me a minimum wage, and in 1987 that was $3.45 an hour, to work there cleaning cars, driving customers to and from the airport, and assisting customers with their car rental contracts. I was also hugely pregnant at the time with Joshua.

Keep in mind that since my parents weren't married anymore, they didn't have to pretend that they liked each other. So, as I return to the office one day after dropping some customers off at the airport, I walk into a heated argument, actually more of a big fight, between my parents. The first thing I see is my sister standing in between them, arms spread out wide, attempting to keep them from physically harming each other. I sigh and think to myself, "Really? Can't we all just get along?" so to speak.

As I enter the office, my mother suddenly removes her shoe from her foot, grasps it tightly, and smacks my dad square in the face with the high heel. Holy Shit! Did that just happen? It had. A small stream of blood ran down his face where the heel punctured his nose. Melita and I are standing there between them with our jaws wide open observing the violence, trying to digest what had just happened. I mean just how angry does a person have to become for it to occur to them to remove the shoe they're currently wearing and use it as a weapon? Right? I fully expected my dad to come completely unglued, but instead, he simply walked to the bathroom and got a tissue to stop the bleeding on his face.

It was about a month later when they both announced Dad was buying out Mom's half of the business. I mean, finally! My dad had his crooked attorney draw up a contract with a bunch of fine print. I told Mom she needed to have her own attorney look at it, but she said she trusted Dad for some reason. I actually believe that my mom always loved my dad. They just could not get along nor live together. So, $100,000. $40,000 down payment, then monthly payments for the rest of it was the deal, or so she thought. In the small print somewhere, it stated that if the business fails or closes, he doesn't have to pay her anymore. He closed down the business a month later. Nice one, Dad.

CHAPTER SIXTEEN

You must be my lucky star
'Cause you make the darkness seem so far
And when I'm lost, you'll be my guide
I just turn around and you're by my side

– Madonna, "Lucky Star"

<u>Lucky</u>
<u>October 1988</u>
<u>Bedford, Texas</u>

"Boy, are you lucky, Lynda. You know that?" my dad smirked at me as we sat in his backyard catching up.
"Oh yeah? How's that Dad?"
"Well, your job. You are so lucky you got that job."
Lucky? I had never been asked on a job interview if I thought I was lucky, and if I had, the answer would have been a resounding NO. Lucky, would have been not getting pregnant in the first place, not landing a good job to support me in spite of it. But I'm pretty sure, at least I think, he was trying to be nice.
"Um, yeah Dad. Super lucky, that's me. Thank you."
"For what?"
Well, exactly.
In a way, he was right though. I started at EDS when I was just 18 as a word processor, typing up sales proposals for the new ATM industry. It was an exciting time to be working in information technology especially in Texas and at EDS, Ross Perot's old company. I would grow up at this company, professionally as well

as personally. I learned so much about the industry from some really amazing people and will always treasure my time there. So okay, lucky.

What was bothering me though was that my dad was saying that all my success so far was just due to dumb luck. I would have to disagree with that statement. I'm pretty sure I was very qualified and did a good job, too. Also, I had attended a secretarial trade school, so I knew what I was doing, and I know I did it well. But thank God for Lady Luck.

CHAPTER SEVENTEEN

I remember I held you so tight
And we danced the night away
With the moves of two wide eyed kids
I need you so much today

– Night Ranger, "When You Close Your Eyes"

Ben
March 1990
Garland, Texas

When I was 19, I found myself in between apartments and so I was staying with friends for a few weeks. It was during this time that I met Brian. It wasn't love at first sight, but there was no denying we had chemistry. Also, during this time, I was taking care of some outstanding issues, like getting my piece of crap car back from my ex-husband. Since I was doing this repo-style while at his workplace, it was going to take an extra set of hands to get the job done.

Brian used to tell this story so much better, but I'll do my best. We had just met through mutual friends, and somehow, they talked him into helping us repossess my Ford POS. Now, I can see that my friends manipulated the situation a little hoping to push Brian and me together, and it worked. Well done, friends! I was attracted to him. As previously mentioned, this car I was repossessing was for all practical purposes, a piece of crap. But I was angry, immature, and spiteful at the time, so I was getting the car back. We found it easily and the second set of keys were ready to go as we ran through the heavy rain to the 1978 LTD POS car. We started it up and got on our way. There really wasn't too much discussion on the way back to our friends' house due to the weather and the condition of the car, which couldn't even pass simple inspection by this time. I glanced over occasionally at him and am pretty sure I saw the horror in his eyes as he did his best to navigate this broken-down cruiser through the flash flood. I have only seen Brian scared twice during his ridiculously short life: Once when I had to tell him he had late-stage lung cancer, and the second was now as he drove us to safety somehow.

We made it back intact to our friends' house despite the never-ending storm. The four of us stood in the dark kitchen since the electricity was out with towels drying ourselves off from the downpour. Since it was storming, and late, and the power's out, our scheming friends suggested him to stay the night. Perfect! Makes sense to everyone.

Brian laid awake on the bed in a spare bedroom listening to the rain and wondering. Wondering if she was thinking about him, too. He thought to himself that this was stupid and he should have driven home instead of thinking about her just one room over. "Ugh," he groaned flipping on his side to face the wall. That's when he heard it. "Creeeek..." the door was opening slowly. Hey, what's this now? Brian feigned sleep while rolling over to face the door, eyes still closed. Then silence. Crap! "Creeeeek," it started up again! Oh Yeah! It was on. He was trying to figure out how to play this cool as he felt the blankets stir by another's movement...

Not being able to wait a moment longer, he opened his eyes widely to find, Ben, the freaking cat staring him in the face, "MEOW!"
"Damn it, Ben!" Brian whispered loudly in frustration, "Get the hell down."

CHAPTER EIGHTEEN

Just hold on loosely
But don't let go
If you cling too tightly
You're gonna lose control

— 38 Special, "Hold on Loosely"

<u>Derwood</u>
<u>1990</u>
<u>Texas</u>

This cowboy, more of a redneck, my sister was living with, and now also the father of her 2-year-old daughter, Heather, was just another cowboy, like all the rest as far as I was concerned that she had dated since high school. There's no accounting for taste, I guess. At any rate, I think his name was Dwayne or Darren or something, so I always referred to him as Derwood.

There were more than a few times when Melita came over with a black eye and emptied out my refrigerator because she was so hungry. This, of course, pissed me smooth off. Excuse me, but where was the badass who used to be my sister? I finally said to her, "Look, just get away from him with Heather and start over. I'm just a phone call away." I guess a month or so later, she called me one evening,

"Hello?" I answered.
"Hey Lynda." It was Melita.

"Hey, what's up?" I inquired.

"Um, just give me a second…" she replied, then paused.

"Sure, okay, take your time." I said waiting.

"So, um, can you come get me?"

"Fuck yes, I can. Where are you?"

She told me where she was. It was a motel in not the best part of town. I don't know why, but I called Brian to tell him I was going to rescue my sister from her current situation. We had only been dating a few months by this time, but I was starting to trust him already for some reason, so that was my first reaction: to call him and tell him what I was about to do.

"Hey Brian, I'm about to go get my sister and her two-year-old in the seedy part of town. Okay? Great! Love ya!" I said quickly as I go to hang up the phone, but before I can, he says,

"Wait! I'll go with you. I think that would be better."

"Okay, sure thing baby." I say thinking if this cutie-pie wants to spend more time with me, awesome! So, I drove to his apartment in a more respectable part of Dallas first, left my car there, and then Brian, Joshua, and I went to retrieve my sister and Heather in the crap part of town in some seedy motel.

I didn't realize that Brian was actually concerned for mine and Josh's safety until we arrived to get Melita and Heather. We drove in his car to get her and I got out once we were in the parking lot. Josh stayed in the car in the backseat. I stood outside the passenger door waiting for Melita and Heather to come down to the car. As I'm standing there, Derwood also exits the motel room and leans against the banister giving me some kind of evil eye. A second later, Brian exits his car from the driver's side and stands up against his car, crossing his arms, looking Derwood directly in the eyes as Melita and Heather make their way toward the car. They reach us, and I help them get their luggage and themselves into Brian's car, then I sit down in the passenger seat and close the car door. Only after seeing that all four of us are securely sitting in the car, Brian opens his driver's side door and sits down.

How was I *not* supposed to love this man?

CHAPTER NINETEEN

We are the crowd
We're coming out
Got my flash on, it's true
Need that picture of you

– Lady GaGa, "Paparazzi"

<u>The Camera</u>
<u>1991</u>
<u>Allen, Texas</u>

Joshua and I were living in our own tiny apartment at this point. A one-bedroom was all I could afford, so I gave my son, four years old at the time, the bedroom and put my bed in the dining area since that's really the only other place I could put it. Josh was, shall we say, a rambunctious child, so his room needed to have a door that I could close. The apartment was only about 700 square feet in total, but I was 20 and supporting myself and my son. It was mine, and I was proud of it. During April one day, I was getting us ready to go to a friend's wedding. I said to my hyper-four-year-old, "Just sit right here and don't move for like twelve to fifteen minutes while I take a shower, okay? Please, Josh." He replied angelically, "Okay Mom!" and smiled at me. He was such a sweet-looking little boy with blond hair and thick glasses but looks can be very deceiving.

So, I'm singing in the shower, lathering up my hair when I hear a loud thump. I whip the shower curtain back to yell out, "Josh!

What was that?" He replies from the exact same spot in the living room, "Nothing, Mother. I didn't hear anything," but I know this kid. As I was getting ready for this wedding, I kept looking around for the damage, but I just didn't see anything out of place. Huh, Weird! Okay, then. I go to retrieve my camera off the kitchen counter so I can take pictures at the wedding. I could have sworn I had a full roll of film (no digital yet), but about 10 pictures had already been taken. Huh, Weird! I think again.

The following week, Brian, Josh, and I are leaving the Target parking lot as I anxiously open my most recent envelope of developed photos including the wedding pictures. Josh is sitting innocently in the back of Brian's 1978 Camaro, looking out the window. I have to say, it was a pretty cool car. Anyway, I'm in the passenger seat as Brian's driving. "Oh, look how pretty she looked, Brian!" I gush. "This is a good one of them both." I go on about how lovely the wedding was and then I'm suddenly confused by the next set of photos. Why would I take a picture of the park in front of my apartment? Huh. The next one was a picture of my apartment from the park. The next was a picture of a ladder and a roofer who was working on our apartment taken right outside my front door, and finally there was an upside-down picture taken from the park from someone who was obviously hanging upside down on the monkey bars. I was fairly confident it wasn't Brian who took those photos, of course. Then, it suddenly occurred to me. The thump I heard when I was showering that day was the front door slamming shut. That little you know what! While I had showered, not only did he not stay put but also he opened and unlocked our front door and decided to go outside and take a few pics, at 4 years of age!

"Joshua, would you like to see some interesting photos?" I asked my son. "Sure, Mom." he replied. I lean back over the front seat to hand him the photos and he starts grinning as he's flipping through them. Then I said, "Remember a couple of weeks ago when we were getting ready to go that wedding?" I asked him casually. "Uh-huh," he replies while still looking through the photos. "Yeah, that was a fun wedding. Hey, what do you think about those pics of the park and our apartment?" I inquired, trying to eventually get my point across to him that he was busted. "Um. Yeah, I like them." Josh replies quietly. "Yeah, you should since you took them." I quipped right back. Then, silence.

The next day Brian came over with his drill and installed a sliding lock way up high on my front door where Josh couldn't reach it. That kid was something else. If only I could lock him up as an adult.

CHAPTER TWENTY

It's got what it takes,
So why can't this be love?

– Van Halen, "Why Can't This be Love"

<u>The Waterbed</u>
<u>1991</u>
<u>Allen, Texas</u>

Brian and I had been dating for about a year when we decided to cohabitate. I had just upgraded to a bigger apartment in anticipation of his imminent arrival and was excited about it.
But the night before he was to move in, I sat there on the phone with him blubbering.
"I don't know. I'm just nervous." I sniffled.
"It's going to be great. I love you and I love Josh. Do you love me?"
He knew I was freaking crazy about him, but I finally eked out very softly, "Yeah."
"So, what's wrong? Do you want me to marry you? I'll marry you, Lynda."
I start crying harder and hyperventilating at his suggestion, sweet as it was.
"NO!! You're making it worse."
He laughed softly and teased, "Well, I've already drained my waterbed, so I'm moving somewhere tomorrow." I could hear the amusement in his voice.
"Oh, well, hell, I guess if you've already drained the bed, then I have no choice but to let you move in." I finally conceded, chuck-

ling myself.

He started talking about how he really meant it, he'd marry me right now if that's what was bothering me. But it actually took another 2 years to convince me to marry him. I was crazy about him, but not so much the actual institution of marriage. But he was an old soul and I sort of loved that about him.

As he's yammering on about marriage, I finally interrupt him, "Could you just (sniffle), you know, stop talking now?"
"Of course, Love," he answered softly, obviously amused.
Somehow, he always had a way of calming me down. God, how I still miss him.

CHAPTER TWENTY-ONE

But whatever road you choose
I'm right behind you, win or lose

– *Rod Stewart, "Forever Young"*

Snickers
1992
Plano, Texas

Joshua was about 5 years old at the time and we were at the Sack N' Save discount grocery store checking out. Brian and I had a full basket of groceries and were heading out to the car as Josh rode in the bottom part of the grocery cart since he thought that was a fun thing to do. Really quick though, isn't it funny how when you're a young couple it's actually fun to go to the grocery store together? Then after about 6 months, nobody wants to run errands anymore, either together or separately? These days, after having been to the grocery store a million times, I get the urge to start hurling cans of corn down the aisle while I'm shopping; I'm just so over of it. Anyway, I digress.

During this particular grocery trip as we make our way out to our car with a full cart of groceries, Josh decides, I have no idea why, to stick his finger in one of the cart's wheels as I'm rolling the cart out to the car, and then starts screaming bloody murder. Really?

His index fingernail had been ripped cleaned off his finger, and all I could think about was that I had dairy products that needed to be refrigerated, but obviously, we were heading to the emergency room (ER), where they were getting to know us by now, "Oh, hello Brian and Lynda, what did Josh do to himself this time?"

Josh was screaming and acting like he had lost an important appendage, so Brian runs back into the store quickly then comes back out with a Snickers bar, "Okay Josh, don't look at your finger. I want you to focus on the deliciousness of this Snickers bar, okay?"
"Um, okay (sniffle)" Josh answered, as I opened the candy bar and gave it to him. Brian was wrapping up Josh's finger with some toilet paper from our recent grocery trip and talking to him at the same time, "Man, that Snickers looks delicious! I should have gotten one for me, too!" Brian said to Josh as he then starts our car heading to the closest emergency room. "Yeah, it's pretty good, I guess." Josh replies while devouring the candy bar, losing interest in his finger injury. I look at Brian as he's driving us to the ER and talking to Josh about the Snickers bar when it occurs to me, "Yeah, it looks like I'm going to have to marry this guy. I have no choice, I love him awful."

CHAPTER TWENTY-TWO

So fathers, be good to your daughters
Daughters will love like you do
Girls become lovers who turn into mothers
So mothers, be good to your daughters, too

– John Mayer, "Daughters"

<u>Daddy's Girl at Last</u>
<u>1998</u>
<u>Allen, Texas</u>

For everything my adoptive father was, my biological father was not. Other than both being Canadian, of course, they didn't have much in common. I was 28 when I sought out my birth mother, but I ended up finding both my mother and father because they were married to each other! I know, so surprising! I thought that was a good sign. When I started searching for my birth Mom, I never expected to find my dad, too! It was and still remains one of the most important relationships of my life.

Where Sid was extremely cheap, and dare I say, greedy, John is nothing but generous. Where Sid would say unkind things to me to break me down, John has always been so supportive and loving; my biggest fan, if you will. John tells me he's proud of me. I honestly can't recall one single time where either of my adoptive parents said they were proud of me. John is my Dad in every way, and I am extremely proud to be his daughter.

Once contact was made through a mediator, we arranged to speak on the phone. I spoke to my Dad first, before my mom. She needed a little more time for the shock to sink in, understandably so. I remember that I was surprised at how deep his voice was. At one point when the conversation stalled, as we were both a bit nervous, he asked me, "So, what do you think of the whole O.J. thing?" Oh yeah, this guy has to be my Dad.

Although he lives in Canada, we maintain a close relationship through visits and phone calls. After all these years, I finally feel like a Daddy's girl and it feels great. It's amazing to feel unconditional love from a parent with no strings attached. Just pure love. Wow. Such a gift I never expected so late in my life. I am eternally grateful to God, or fate, or whatever it is that brought us back together.

CHAPTER TWENTY-THREE

Another one bites the dust, yeah
Hey, I'm gonna get you too
Another one bites the dust

– Queen, "Another One Bites the Dust"

<u>Busted</u>
<u>2002</u>
<u>Allen, Texas</u>

I've always had trouble sleeping due to my numerous medical issues, so one night about 2 a.m. I stood looking out my bedroom window. Josh's room was right next to us and at this time he was about 15 years old. As I stood there in silence, I heard odd movement and zippers being opened and closed like on luggage in Josh's room, so I went down the hall and stood outside his door so I could listen better. I could see him moving about his room from the dim light coming out from the bottom of his door. What the heck is he doing? Then I heard the zipper of a bag close once more I suppose. Huh. Then, I heard the window slide open. Oh, that little fucker. I ran downstairs as quietly as I could and stood by the back door in the kitchen as his room was directly above. I'm watching out the window of the backdoor and suddenly a duffel bag drops to the ground. Uh-huh. Oh, he's gonna get it. I wait about 5 seconds, then open the door quietly and look up.

I saw him with one leg out the window, and I look at up and say, "Dude, you are so busted." He replies, "Oh, um, I was just going for a walk." like I'm an idiot. "Uh-huh. What's the bag for?"
"Oh, it's just a sweater in case I get cold." Josh explains.
"I see. So, you decided to take a walk at three a.m. by sneaking out your window and taking a duffel bag full of I don't know what yet, and you actually expect me to believe this nonsense? You do know that you are totally busted, yes?"
"Yeah", he replies he crawls back in the window.

The next day, Brian swings Josh's bedroom door wide open, a startled Josh looks at him with wide eyes. He says nothing but has his drill in his hand and some 2-inch screws in his mouth. "Whir, whir!" Brian walks in with the noisy drill and goes directly to the window and begins nailing Josh's bedroom window shut using his drill. I'm standing at the door enjoying the show when Josh looks at me with panic in his eyes and pleads, "What if there's a fire or something?" I shrug my shoulders standing there with my arms crossed and reply casually, "Yeah, you know how to get out of this house. If all else fails and there's a fire then throw a chair through the window. You'll be okay." Josh is sitting there looking at us as though we had both just lost our minds. Sometimes being a parent was just good, old-fashioned fun.

CHAPTER TWENTY-FOUR

Ireland I am coming home
I can see your rolling fields of green
And fences made of stone
I am reaching out, won't you take my hand
I'm coming home Ireland

– Garth Brooks, "Ireland"

<u>The Luck of the Irish</u>
<u>1999</u>
<u>Texas/Ireland</u>

My mom, Mary, was simply the best. Considering her sixth-grade education, she did remarkably well for herself. She left her home in Ireland at 16 to go to England and became a nanny. This was her way out of the poverty she was born into. She worked hard and became a very successful small business owner. At one time, we lived in a motel my parents owned, and they had a car rental agency as well. Not bad for a sixth-grade education. But her biggest accomplishments were, without a doubt, being a mother and a grandmother.

Mom was born in the very small town of Ballymahon in County Longford, Ireland. Ballymahon is what I would call, quaint. Mom would call it poor, but nevertheless, this is still where most of her family resides which is why she had planned a trip home for her 65th birthday. I remember being a little worried about her before she even left on this trip. Something didn't feel right, but I told myself I was just being paranoid. It's a long journey getting to Ireland from America and she was getting older and traveling alone. About a week before her departure, my mom felt compelled to show me where she kept her will and other important papers, "just in case." Was my mother also worried about this trip? She would also repeat to me several times before leaving, "This is my last time to travel home; it's getting too hard." Indeed, it was about to become very hard.

The day after my mom departed for her trip home, my phone rang at 4 a.m. In my experience, 4 a.m. calls are never good news, and this was no exception; I wasn't wrong. My Uncle Pat was calling from Ireland. He was saying a lot and saying it quickly, but I understood him when he said, "Yer mum's in hospital, yea, with a bleedin' brain! Can ye come Lynda?" Well, of course. Of course, I'm coming; it's my mama.

I'd like to take a moment here to remind everyone with family in other countries just how important it is to either get a passport or keep it current if you already have one. Because as it was, I was the only one with a current passport, so I was traveling to Ireland alone. So, to recap, I was 29 years old and flying to a faraway foreign land all by myself to meet up with family I had never met nor really spoken to so that I could get to my mother who may, or may not, be alive by the time I get there. Awesome! This is the frame of mind I'm in as I board the plane to fly to Dublin, anxious and scared. Naturally, the plane is full of happy-go-lucky Americans, most of whom probably had saved up for this trip of a lifetime, I'm guessing by their "Kiss Me, I'm Irish" t-shirts and the sequined shamrocks on their headbands. I find my seat and wait for the ride of a lifetime.

When I finally arrived in Dublin, after two layovers, I had been awake for over 24 hours. I was scared and exhausted as I scanned the crowd for pretty much *anyone* that at least resembled my Mother. Bingo. Four older women that looked a lot like my mom were seated by luggage retrieval. I timidly walked up to them, "Aunt Lizzie?" I inquired tentatively. Suddenly all four ladies were on their feet and rushing me, "Ohhhhh Lynda!" I heard in unison. Yes, definitely my Aunts. "Come on now... We're off to ye hospital straight away now. She's been awake!" My Aunt Lizzie positively glowed as if my mom had just finished the Ironman triathlon.

After all the travel and rushing around, once I got to the hospital all activity just stopped. The jet lag didn't help either, and now I was frustrated with a foreign medical system that I didn't understand. She had endured 1 of about 10 brain surgeries to come so far, and I was frantically waiting to finally see her in a very small waiting room down the hall from the neurological ward.

The public hospital in Dublin was a real head trip for me. Not only was my mother barely clinging to life but I felt like Alice in Wonderland. Where the hell AM I? I was quite used to the polite doctors and professional hospital staff in America, not surgeons who referred to themselves as Mister instead of Doctor, and nuns for nurses and the lack of communication actually boggled my mind. After my mother's surgery, I was hoping to talk to the surgeon, Mr. Pigeon (see what I mean?). Normally, in the United States, you can expect the doctor to address the family after a very dangerous surgery. Well, not in Ireland. I sat outside this man's office on the floor in the hall for 4 hours waiting to pounce on him as he left his office one night so I could try to get some answers on my mom's condition. When the door finally opened, I jumped up and immediately addressed him, "Mr. Pigeon! Mr. Pigeon, can I please have just a moment of your time? I'm Mary's daughter, the American? You know, she just about died yesterday?"
"Yes."
"Well, uh... um." I started crying right at that moment. And he just

stood there. He didn't offer any information or any words of comfort.

"When can I take my mom home?" I finally managed to get out.

"There's NO way she can travel. We don't even know if she'll get through the next day."

"Uh-huh. Okay. So, what's the plan?"

"Brain traumas are very unpredictable, so we just have to wait and see."

Wait and see? Not one of my strengths, but he was right. I was going to have to return home without her, and the guilt was overwhelming.

When I finally saw her, I thought to myself that she actually looked pretty good. She came around for a few minutes and opened her eyes, and we all became super excited. Aunt Lizzie started gushing all over her, "Look whose here Mary!" referring to me.

My mother nodded her head.

"Do you know who this is?" Lizzie asked my mom.

Again, a positive nod.

"Who is it?" Lizzie asked her much more softly.

"My mother," my mom said.

"Fuck" I said.

Ten days later, I sat in the Dublin airport terminal waiting to board the plane back to America. My Aunt Kitty had dropped me at the airport and assured me they would take care of my mom and keep in constant communication with me regarding her condition. I couldn't believe I was leaving her behind in Ireland, still in such critical health. Again, not a big public crier, but I sat in that stupid airport terminal and just sobbed before boarding the plane, leaving my mother behind.

CHAPTER TWENTY-FIVE

Oh the yellow rose of Texas is the only girl I love
Her eyes are even bluer than Texas skies above
Her heart's as big as Texas and whenever I may go
I'll remember her forever because I love her so

– Elvis Presley, "The Yellow Rose of Texas"

<u>Back to Texas</u>
<u>February–October 1999</u>
<u>Texas</u>

Throughout the next 10 months, I became very close with my family in Ireland, in particular my Aunt Lizzie and her daughter, my cousin, Mary (my mom's namesake). They were my only source of communication on Mom's condition, which had stagnated at this point. Because of the bleeding in her brain, the doctors needed to implant a stint so the spinal fluid could flow normally again. But every single time they did brain surgery to install this stint, she would end up getting infected, so they'd have to remove it. Finally, after 10 attempts the doctors in Ireland just stopped trying altogether. My mother was in sort of a coma; basically, she was unconscious due to all the fluid on her brain. For 10 months as she wasted away and her muscles atrophied, I was worried. In addition, Mary was becoming concerned about her own mother, my Aunt Lizzie. She explained to me that

Aunt Lizzie had become obsessed with my mom's condition. Apparently, it's all she spoke or thought about. She was also seeking out psychic mediums who would assure her everything would work out and then declared that yes, your sister will walk out of that hospital! Right. Then they would charge her their $100 fee and encourage her to come back soon. Yeah, I bet. It was getting to them and it wasn't right that Mary was so worried about her own mother who was obsessing over my mother. I had to figure out how to get her back to Texas.

After about nine months into this, I was lying in bed recovering from sinus surgery when it occurred to me that there has to be somebody, somewhere in this damn country that can stand up for my mother. My mom, who had paid taxes her entire life and donated to charities and was a respectable member of society. Right? The problem at hand now was the insurance company. What a surprise. Remember, I said she was going home for her 65th birthday? The day her policy went into effect is the very same day she had the aneurysm burst in her brain, and the insurance company was claiming her policy was invalid. Of course. What insurance company with an ounce of common sense would want to pay for 10 brain surgeries, a 10-month hospital stay in a foreign country, as well as figure out how to get her back to America? It was much easier and much less expensive for them to come up with a reason to cancel her policy. But they were wrong, and I knew it.

The Health Care Finance Administration (HCFA) is the agency that monitors health insurance companies in America. After researching for a few hours, I finally found it along with about 60 e-mail addresses to various department executives. I sent the same letter to all of them outlining my mom's situation. A week later, I received a call from just one of the executives, but one was all it took.

"Lynda, we're going to get your mother home." Finally, I literally broke down at my desk at work and just sobbed, but they were tears of relief. Once HCFA gave their ruling to this particular health insurance company, things started happening.

Since Mom was still completely comatose, she would be getting home by private air ambulance. Oh, I really understood now why they didn't want to cover this bill. In 1999, the Lear jet that would bring my mom home was a $50,000 private flight that would carry a pilot, a nurse, and my mom who would remain on a stretcher. I was told they would refuel in Iceland, Montreal and then arrive at Dallas/Fort Worth International Airport. At that point, customs would board the plane to go over all her documents. Then, she would be loaded onto a regular ambulance and driven to Baylor hospital in Dallas where I had managed to get her into an amazing rehabilitation program specifically for brain trauma patients.
I was already waiting for her at Baylor hospital when I saw the ambulance pull up. I had not seen her in 7 months since I last visited Ireland. It was hard to believe she was actually here after all this time. The first thing which was done at Baylor hospital was to get her into surgery to implant the stint. Immediately after the fluid on her brain was drained, she became conscience. She came out of surgery with a lot to say, although she was extremely confused. But again, at least she was wide awake. Since she had been unconscious for the previous 10 months, the muscles in her legs atrophied and she would never walk again. Now, this was extremely frustrating to me because it was completely preventable. Mom should have been receiving some basic physical therapy as she laid there in a coma to at least try to prevent muscle atrophy, but 10 months without any therapy was just too little, too late. So, Ireland, not understanding her insurance situation, put her on the waitlist for public health to receive physical therapy, but she never cleared the list. So, although my mother was not technically paralyzed, she could no longer walk and that was nothing compared to her brain trauma.

Unless you've ever had to care for a relative with brain trauma, you just can't understand how the entire dynamic of your relationship is nothing at all like it was, pretrauma. Suddenly, the parent becomes the child, and the child becomes the parent. Sometimes, Mom would look at me with disdain and disgust when I suggested her to do something unreasonable, like say, brush her teeth. Unfortunately, rehabilitation wasn't doing a lot for my mom either. She would refuse therapy or she'd give them nothing but hell if any of the therapists could get her to participate.

Woven throughout all the other areas of my life were my weekend visits to my mom in her nursing home as she lingered for the next 11 years until her death in 2009 when her heart stopped one morning after breakfast. At last, she was finally freed from her own personal prison. She didn't have much family here and it seemed to mean an awful lot to her sisters, so I had her remains sent home to Ireland, where my Aunts laid her to rest properly.

CHAPTER TWENTY-SIX

Those times I waited for you seem so long ago,
I wanted you far too much to ever let you go,
You know you never get by, I feel it too
And I guess I never could stand to lose
It's such a pity to say, goodbye to you

– Scandal, "Goodbye to You"

<u>The Day the Sky Fell</u>
<u>February 2006</u>
<u>Allen, Texas</u>

February first was Rachel's, my daughter, 10th birthday. As usual, we had a small birthday party with pizza and cake for family and close friends. Something unusual caught my attention–Brian's family all commented on how he had lost some weight and was looking good. But I knew neither his diet nor activity level had changed, so it actually caught my attention. Not willing to go there mentally, I dismissed the thought as quickly as I had it. True, he was getting over a chest cold, but no way, he's 38 years old. It couldn't be.

Over the next 2 weeks, the chest cold actually seemed to get worse. He'd go to the ER complaining of a cough and that he was short of breath, and they would give him antibiotics, an inhaler and send him on his way. Finally, it got to the point where he couldn't walk 10 feet without being completely out of breath and was sleeping 18 hours out of 24. Also, he wasn't looking so good. I called our doctor and demanded to run some tests because something was not right. They ran some blood work and then called me at work, "Take him to the hospital immediately. His liver and kidneys are about to completely shut down," the nurse instructed me. I was terrified because I knew something was catastrophically wrong. They admitted him and I went home for the evening. The next morning, he was calling me on my cell phone telling me to come and get him. I could hear him struggling for breath and he sounded confused as well. I said, "Brian, I can't just come get you. We have to figure out what's wrong. I want you to ring the bell for the nurse, and tell them you aren't breathing well and I'm on my way up there."

Fifteen minutes later, I walked into his room. He was laying back and struggling for breath. I looked at the monitor, and his blood pressure was 80 over 50. What the fuck? I ran out of his room and down the hall to the nurses' station, "WHY can't he breathe? His blood pressure is eighty over fifty!" Suddenly, nurses go running down the hall. Then they rush him just as quickly to the ICU and one of the nurses tells me his doctor will be out to talk to me just as soon as she can.

The doctor finally emerges and tells me that my husband is very sick. Frankly, he's about to crash and they can't figure out why. She says they have about 10 specialists concurrently working on him trying to figure it out. But in the meanwhile, he's using too much energy to try to breathe, so they were sedating him and putting him on a respirator to preserve his strength to fight. There's talk of transferring him to Baylor Dallas to get him in the organ transplant unit as soon as possible, although they're still not sure why his organs are failing. Hours go by and I wait and wait and wait. She comes out about 11 p.m. to tell me they are still figuring it out. She says he has to be exhausted because she's his doctor and she was exhausted. That remains the only time I've ever heard a doctor say that to me about anyone.

Finally, about midnight, she comes out with some actual information. The cardiologist was studying his scans for the third time and thought the area around his heart was slightly enlarged so they were going to do an electrocardiogram. The cardiologist then comes out to explain they know what's going on. The sac around his heart, the pericardium sac, is bursting with fluid. This is not normal. It usually only occurs with tuberculosis (TB) or cancer, and let's be honest, when was the last time there was a TB pandemic? They were taking him into surgery to drain the sac and the fluid would be checked for cancer cells. Several hours later, he's out of surgery and although his organs are beginning to work again now that his heart can pump blood properly, they give me the news. Cancer. And it's really bad.

He's in recovery but we're far from done for the night. They have to perform dialysis on his blood because its so dirty by this point, it's almost toxic. Also, they told me they are going to keep him sedated and on a respirator for a while, so his body can continue to heal without struggling to breathe. I sleep in a chair for the next few hours. I can't leave, not that I want to, but because they had no way to predict what was going to need to happen, they needed right there in case there were more consent forms to sign. And the oncologist wants to meet with me the next morning to go over everything. The sky just fell.

I sit in his office and prepare myself.

The doctor speaks, "There's no easy way to say this. It's in both lungs and his brain, and that's just what we know of at this moment. If he's lucky he may have up to three months to live..." the oncologist keeps talking but I don't hear anything else.

"Wait. He's only thirty-eight." I argue as if this will make a difference in his diagnosis. "I'm sorry. I truly am," he replies. Uh no, that just won't do, I'm thinking as I feel the panic well up inside of me.

Later, I sit outside while my friends try to tell me that no matter what, I'll be okay. I know they were only trying to help, but they just didn't understand. You know what? YOU go be okay. I'll never be okay again. Your husbands are alive and have a future. I'm 36 and we have two small girls, and none of this shit show works without him! I'm convinced, I'm being punished by God for something awful I must have done.

CHAPTER TWENTY-SEVEN

That last kiss, I'll cherish
Until we meet again, and time makes it harder
I wish I could remember,
But I keep your memory
You visit me in my sleep
My Darling, who knew?

– Pink, "Who Knew"

<u>Worst Day of My Life</u>
<u>August 24, 2006</u>
<u>Allen, Texas</u>

I walked in through the garage door to our home after a long day at work and Brian wasn't on the couch like he normally used to be, so I ran upstairs to our bedroom and found him in our bed; he's awake but he tells me it hurts to breathe. I replied anxiously that I would go get his morphine, but he shakes his head and says it's worse than that. We need to call 911. The paramedics arrived and had to get him down our stairs in a chair because the stupid stairs we had were curved, but then they got him on the stretcher. All of our neighbors are outside watching the show, but we were good friends with most of them, so I left Rachel and Abby with one of the neighbors, and then followed the ambulance to the hospital in McKinney, which was the closest trauma center and there was something definitely traumatic going on.

Once we're at the hospital and he's been examined, it's determined that his entire left lung is full of blood, a huge pulmonary embolism being the correct medical term. This is common in people with advanced lung disease, like Brian. He's really struggling to breathe by this point so they sedate him and put him on a respirator to breathe for him. Before he goes under, I bend down to his ear and say, "I love you. We did this before and we'll do it again." He nods, so I know he heard me. That was the last thing I ever said to my husband.

They do have treatment options for healthy people who develop pulmonary embolisms, but he was so very sick that these options wouldn't work for him. There's medication they can administer but this medication would cause the tumors in his brain to bleed so he would hemorrhage immediately and die. Surgery is also another option, but there wasn't a surgeon alive willing to operate on him because he was so close to death; he just wouldn't make it through surgery at this point. So, the nice doctor explained to me that tonight would be the night my husband was going to die because pulmonary embolisms are not compatible with life. The doctor asks me to sign a DNR form and that grabs my attention.
"What?" I asked.
"We need you to sign a DNR."
"Well, no."
"Ma'am, your husband will not make it through the night. There's nothing we can do for him."
"Well, so be it, but I'm not signing that. He's fought with everything he has for the last six months and signing that would be an insult to him. So, no. And please don't call me ma'am" and I walk away.

I'm on the main floor of the hospital lobby waiting for Josh to arrive when I hear over the loudspeaker, "Code Blue! Code Blue in the ICU! All available personnel to ICU!" and I just know. I just *know* it's him. So, I race back up to ICU and I can see what looks like a dozen people working on him trying to resuscitate him, but it's not working. After about 20 minutes one of the doctors walks out to me to tell me they're going to stop now, they can't bring him back. God was ready for him.

I'm not sure which was worse, watching him die or having to tell our girls he had died. Our poor babies were only 5 and 10 at the time. Joshua was 19, but hell, it was bad for all of us. I left the hospital without Brian and it felt so wrong, but somehow drove home feeling very numb. I guess I was in shock or something. It was 4:30 a.m. when I got home so I slept for a few hours before calling the neighbors to get my girls. I was emotionally spent and slept hard, but not long.

"Hi Robin. He didn't make it." I said to my neighbor on the phone. I heard her gasp lightly, "Okay, I'll bring them on over now." she replied with tears in her voice. "Yep, okay." I said and hung up. I walked to the front door and opened it. I saw my girls' faces and when Rachel saw my face, she ran straight to me screaming and crying, "Nooooooo! No, No, NO!" All I could do was hold her and whisper how sorry I was, and tell her how much I loved her. Abby was so young she didn't even understand death yet, but she clung to my legs realizing something very bad had happened. We were irreconcilably broken.

CHAPTER TWENTY-EIGHT

It's no surprise to me, I am my own worst enemy
'Cause every now and then, I kick the living shit out of me
The smoke alarm is going off and there's a cigarette,
Still burning

– Lit, "My Own Worst Enemy"

<u>The Dark Years: Burning Bridges</u>
<u>2006–2016</u>
<u>Texas</u>

At 36 years of age when Brian made me a widow, I entered a period of time that I refer to as the dark years. For a solid 10 years, I fell into a deep depression fueled by addiction and anger. The day he died, time became the enemy for me. I wished I could just stop time because life went on around me without him, and it sucked. It wasn't fair that the world went on spinning without him and at this time, my only wish was to join him. Our family did not work without him, and my behavior was only making things worse. But my grief was a deep dark hole and I just wanted to stay there forever. However, I had three really good reasons that kept me from taking my own life: Josh, Rachel, and Abby. At the time of his death, they were 19, 10, and 5, respectively.

In the Fall of 2005, I had my first back surgery, and in February

2006, Brian was diagnosed with late-stage lung cancer. By this time, I was fully immersed in "pain management." This is during the time when a particular pharmaceutical company was pushing out OxyContin like candy. I received a shit-ton of narcotics every month. It was just too easy for me. It made me feel warm and euphoric instead of sad and suicidal. Even as addiction took everything else away from me, I clung to those stupid pills like a lifeline when in reality they were taking everything I had worked so hard for. I burned every bridge I had.

I had no interest in anything except getting high and forgetting as much as I possibly could. I also began to isolate myself. I just didn't feel like socializing with anyone other than my pill bottle. No good to anyone at this time, I lost friends I'd had for years. In retrospect, they must have known I was abusing my medication and so had no choice but to cut ties with me. Believe me, I get it.

I had worked very hard my entire life and built a solid career as a highly respected Executive Assistant in the IT industry, and I was destroying that, too. I ended up quitting my last job in the corporate world because I was, deservingly so, about to get fired. I didn't even bother looking for work after that. My health had begun to deteriorate as well by this time, so I never went back to work in corporate America. My husband, my friends, my house, my finances, my career, my self-respect, and my sanity, I had lost it all.

CHAPTER THIRTY

*No pain, inside
You're my protection
But how do I feel this good sober?*

– Pink, "Sober"

<u>The Fallout</u>
<u>2017</u>
<u>Fort Worth, Texas</u>

Once I was clearheaded for the first time in 10 years, it was time to sit down and take a long, hard good look at everything my addiction caused. It wasn't pretty. By this time, my children are adults and the foggy warm haze of narcotics had cleared, I felt so much remorse for what I had put them through. When you are amid addiction, it justifies your every move so if you hurt your loved ones in the name of getting your fix, so be it. Addiction is at the very core, selfish. That thought alone fills me with shame. How dare I take my children for granted for even one moment when they are my entire reason for living? How dare I play with such a precious gift from God? It was time to rebuild, create my new normal, again.

I have vague memories of the numerous times I was high. Memories of doing stupid things, like eating a stick of butter, or "nodding off" and falling off the toilet because I was so jacked up. Hell, falling down in general. And that's just what I remember. Obviously, this did not make me mother of the year.

But I would have to say my biggest mistake at this time was the marriage I had entered into. You know how we always blow off the instructions our doctors give us? Like, for example, do not sign any kind of legal document while under the influence of narcotics? I did that. I signed a marriage license and remarried in 2008 in a sad way of escaping my grief I suppose. In my current state, I thought marriage equals happiness because I had been SO happy with Brian, but silly me. It does not mean that you can just marry anyone and be happy. I mean, come on. It doesn't work that way, and deep down I knew it. So back to assessing the damage. No job, no friends, no money, and I was in a marriage that clearly did not work. My actual real health issues were also coming to light now that I wasn't just masking the pain. Ironically, with all of my medical issues, I'd be the perfect candidate for pain management. How freaking funny is that? But I know better now. Even though the medical community would gladly throw narcotics my way, I can't. I can never go back to being dependent on any kind of chemical. I honestly don't think I would survive it again.

Something I had to come to terms with is that I had married a man just like my adoptive father. I mean they are so similar it's downright scary. Both were unreasonable, full of rage, violence, and bigotry. It was bad, and I had exposed my girls to this during their very important formative years. Fuck! It was going to be a bitch putting my life back together, but I had earned it.

CHAPTER TWENTY-NINE

My eyes feel like they're gonna bleed
Dried up and bulging out of my skull
My mouth is dry, my face is numb
Fucked up and spun out in my room

– Green Day, "Brain Stew"

<u>Detox</u>
<u>June 2016</u>
<u>Fort Worth, Texas</u>

If addiction was an evil demon that possessed me, then withdrawal is the Devil, itself. There was this indescribable internal war raging between my body and my brain. And my brain had been justifying opioids to my body for the last 10 years. So, weak and pathetic really doesn't adequately describe how weak and pathetic I was. Ideally, detoxification from drugs or alcohol should take place under medical supervision, but this was a luxury I just didn't have access to. I suppose I could have gone to the hospital, but I honestly couldn't make it to the bathroom most of the time during detox, so I preferred to wait there for the peacefulness of death that was surely coming for me. That's how I felt anyway.

I really planned for this, kicking and screaming all the way of course, but I knew I couldn't put it off any longer. I stocked up on Gatorade, water, soup, crackers, Aleve, and Imodium before taking my last pill. I also had to prepare myself for the onslaught of physical pain which I had simply been masking for the last 10 years. I called my pain management doctor's office and told them I wouldn't be back, effectively cutting myself off.

I prepared my children in advance for the event informing them that I wouldn't be available for anything, like don't bother me. In other words, unless you're prepared to perform an Exorcism on me while I detox, you probably just want to stay away. Also, probably not a bad idea to have a Priest on speed dial, just in case.

At my worst, I was crushing up my pills and snorting them. It hits your system faster that way. I had little straws hidden all over the place. I had been prescribed 120 mg of morphine a day, as well as up to four 30 mg tablets of oxycodone per day; however, I usually took more than that. My tolerance was extremely high by this time so this detox was hell.

On day three or four, Abby, my youngest, opened my door just slightly to see if I was still, indeed, alive. One of my tennis shoes sailed through the air toward her but hit the wall, 10 inches to the left of her face. "Get out. Don't talk to me." I muttered miserably.

Abby immediately closed the door and contemplated if she should go get the Priest, ultimately deciding against it. She actually told me much later on that she had absolutely no faith in me that I would ever stop. When I told her that I was going to detox, she said okay, but was actually thinking, "Yeah, right, Mom. Pfffft, as if." This made me so sad, but she said that once I did detox, she was thrilled to get her Mom back. I didn't even know I was missing, so this was exciting news to me too, but you get my meaning.

I started to actually get out of bed on day five or six. By day 10, I was even starting to get a small appetite back. Soon after this, I woke up one morning and realized that I was getting there. That thought made me smile for the first time in a very long time.

CHAPTER THIRTY-ONE

If you're lost you can look and you will find me
Time after time
If you fall I will catch you, I'll be waiting
Time after time

– Cyndi Lauper, "Time After Time"

<u>Melita</u>
<u>2018</u>
<u>Texas</u>

My sister was adopted in 1976 when I was six years old and she was 10. She was a Native, as they are referred to in Canada, so she was exotically beautiful and tall with dark brown hair and eyes. I thought she was fascinating, and she was. She would tell me the most fantastic stories of her early childhood in Newfoundland. I wanted to be just like her, and she somehow looked out for me almost instinctively. Not bound by blood, but by circumstance, our bond was unbreakable. We became sisters in Canada, moved to the States with our parents, and always, *always* had each other's back.

One day in April 2018, I answered my phone and it was Melita. She had been unexpectedly hospitalized the night before. "What's wrong?" I asked anxiously. "Colon cancer" was all she replied, and I immediately felt my stomach fall out of my butt. My one true ally was dying and I was instantly devastated. "No. No, you don't." was all I could manage to say.

Melita was one of *the* funniest people I have ever known. I can't tell you how many hours we spent laughing together. Sometimes, I think we laughed for fear of crying, but one copes as one must. The next day after getting the bad news, I sat in her hospital room with her daughters, Heather and Chelsea, awaiting her surgery to remove most of her colon. We were all very somber not really speaking when Melita piped up suddenly, "Heather! Heather, I got the cancer." she said with a goofy smile on her face, quoting *Forrest Gump.* Heather shrieked, "Mom! Stop!" Of course, Melita and I sat there stifling our giggles. Even in her darkest hour, she was trying to put *us* at ease with humor.

She never left the hospital and 2 weeks later she passed away of sepsis from complications due to the surgery. I had lost the very best friend I ever had.

A few months later, I received a copy of my sister's death certificate in the mail from my niece, Heather. Heather is Melita's oldest daughter and was her official next of kin at the time of her death. My niece's father, Melita's ex-husband, Roy, showed up inexplicably at the hospital during my sister's dying process. I guess to provide comfort to Heather and Chelsea. I never liked him, so I just tried to keep my distance from him. I'm sorry, but there's dumb, and then there's ignorant. He was both. Allow me to explain how I came to this obvious conclusion.

As my sister takes her last breath, too many people are in the room. I kept thinking she wouldn't like a crowd like this, but I wasn't in charge, Heather was. But Heather was just a blubbering mess in her Father's arms as Melita passed. Suddenly, he announces to everyone, like he's her savior, "Don't worry, I'll take care of everything." Okay. Well, everything really can encompass an awful lot, so what are we talking about here? After we were all ushered out of the room and into the hospital corridor, I attempted to ask Roy, you know, like what the hell? "Don't worry about a thing, Lynda, I'm taking care of everything." he says to me as he quickly exits the hospital. I do not feel reassured.

So, as I review the information on Melita's death certificate, I start shaking my head. I knew it. I freaking KNEW it! He can't take care of shit because he's a stupid, ignorant, red-neck idiot! And I knew this. I should have known better. Where her maiden name and parents' names were supposed to be listed, instead it read, "UNKNOWN." What the actual fuck? What man doesn't know his ex-wife's maiden name? Or her parents' names? Furthermore, how hard is it to find out? Just ask one of your kids for Pete's sake! I mean this really takes a special kind of stupid. Under normal circumstances, it might not have angered me so much. But this was Melita. She may have been an orphan when she was a small child, but she did not die one. She was a Kozar. We were four rejects were brought together by fate, and like us or not, we were the effin' Kozars. I am absolutely mortified to think that anyone in the future researching their family tree will run across Melita's death certificate and dismiss her as a poor little orphan. She was not an orphan, damn it.

CHAPTER THIRTY-TWO

You better turn me loose
You better set me free
Cuz I'm hot young running free
A little bit better than I used to be

– Motley Crue, "Live Wire"

<u>Prologue</u>
<u>Starting Over</u>
<u>No Where Yet, Texas</u>

Starting over at 50 just isn't something I pictured I'd ever have to do. It was, however, a necessary and natural consequence of addiction and excess. And, not to offend any active or recovering addicts, but addicts are the most selfish people to roam our planet because addiction, itself, is selfish. This is the very nature of the condition.

When recovering from addiction, you are forced to confront all the horrible things you did to your loved ones while active in your addiction, all in the name of healing. This was going to be one long list, and my children were at the top of it. When you've destroyed your life, and in the process shattered the lives of your loved ones, it becomes one daunting task. Alcoholics Anonymous refers to this as "taking an honest moral inventory of yourself." I'm ashamed of so many things on my list, but as I recover, I am slowly learning to forgive myself. I still don't feel like I deserve my children's forgiveness, but they forgave so easily and willingly. They are the light at the end of my tunnel, my reason for being.

Two of my three children are also addicts. I live with this stark reality every day since my memories are no longer numbed by opioids. By birth, exposure, or both, two of them are addicts. One of them is not. I believe that we, as a society, have to do better when it comes to addiction. It simply destroys lives. And I firmly believe that the opioid epidemic in America was or still is a disgrace. I know because I fell victim to it. Although the much stricter more recent prescribing practices are now in place, it displaced many pain patients forcing them to go to heroin now that the doctors who had been giving it to them willingly all along and even recommending it to them, cut them off suddenly due to the new federal laws in place. Fine for the doctor, but for the patient who was now already chemically dependent on narcotics, where did that leave them? Many went to heroin, and believe me I considered it. But for me, I knew if I went down that road, I might as well grab a loaded gun and blow my brains out. So, somehow, by the Grace of God, I dug down deep and decided to detox on my own and followed through with it, which you should know by now if you've read this far.

If there's one thing I've definitely learned from my first 50 years is that John Lennon said it all when he said, "Life is what happens when you're busy making plans." I've also realized that without darkness, there is no light. Perhaps I wouldn't appreciate the simple things that I do so very much if I had not had the dark times to compare them to? The day I married Brian and had "planned" on being married to him for the next 50 or 60 years, never could I have ever dreamed that I would only get to have him for 13 of the best years of my life. Even so, no especially so, I am extremely grateful for every second I spent loving him. Just as I am equally grateful to have had such an amazing sister to grow up with and love, as well. Even through the tragedies, I learned important life lessons. I am grateful for it all. I am also hopeful for a bright future, come what may.

DIRTY LITTLE SECRETS

ACKNOWLEDGEMENT

Special thanks to numerous friends and family for taking the time to review edit after edit after edit after edit...

Amelia Alderson
Roger Alderson
Tricia Bavol
Maureen Jones
Pam MacDonald
Vincent Soto

Among many others.

ABOUT THE AUTHOR

Elle Soto

Elle Soto is a poet, writer and the author of "Dirty Little Secrets: Life, Love, Adoption and Addiction", a collection of short stories and lessons learned. Drawing from her own personal history, she creates a unique experience for her readers finding the fine line between humor and tragedy in some of life's more difficult lessons. She is a lifelong writer and began documenting events in her life as a teenager. Elle lives and works out of her home in Arlington, Texas. She has three grown children, a dachshund and sings out loud every single chance she gets.

ElleSototheAuthor@gmail.com

Printed in Great Britain
by Amazon